Whispers of Eden

Whispers of Eden

*A Collection of Adolescent Poetry
and Short Stories (1980–1990)*

Shannyn R. Snyder

Writers Club Press
New York Lincoln Shanghai

Whispers of Eden
A Collection of Adolescent Poetryand Short Stories (1980–1990)

Writers Club Press
an imprint of iUniverse, Inc.

For information address:
iUniverse, Inc.
2021 Pine Lake Road, Suite 100
Lincoln, NE 68512
www.iuniverse.com

ISBN: 0-595-27187-1

Printed in the United States of America

To dream is to open up your mind to unique possibilities. To believe is to create new paths in your life's road. To fantasize is to utilize the power of the mind to imagine who or what may one day become reality.

For the whispers of Eden, and other such joys she brings to my life, this—my first book—is dedicated to my daughter. I love you, sweet girl.

—Mommy

Contents

Poems of Family 1

Beautiful 2

Understanding 7

Family 8

Nana's Song 9

The Attic 10

Remembrance 11

Our Road 12

Dad 13

Gramma 14

On Your Birthday 15

Childhood Ballad 16

Friend 17

Daddy 18

Not Forever 19

Concrete Poem for Mom 20

A Brother's Goldfish 21

The Fight 22

Support 23

Poems of Fear 24

Winter Ghost 25

Dying 37

Nightmare *38*

Attack *40*

Abuse *41*

Break Up *42*

Crumbling Walls *43*

Footprints *44*

Tears *45*

Long Distance *46*

Ethiopia *47*

Plea for Peace *48*

Lonely House *49*

Break in *50*

War *52*

Moon Shadows *53*

FOG *54*

Poems of Faith 55

Why I Walk *56*

Confusion *59*

Calvary *60*

Grace *61*

Let Your Light Shine *62*

We Will Stand *63*

In Him *64*

Symbol *65*

Promised Land *67*

Witness *69*

Worthwhile *70*

Contents

Poems of Hope 71

WWII's Aging Heroes 73

Eden 75

Stained Glass 76

Trusting You 78

My Future 79

Overseas Flight 80

Lighthouse 81

See This in Me 82

Heaven 84

The Unicorn 86

Ready 87

Together 88

One Day 89

Destroyed Love 90

Save the Children 91

Coming Home 92

From a Soldier 93

Tortured Heart 95

A Prayer 96

Safe 98

Granted Taken 99

Dedication Enclosed 100

Tell Me 101

Forget It 102

DIVERSION 104

Metamorphosis 105

It's Late 106

Sunrise *107*

Wonderful *108*

Race *109*

Waves *110*

Poverty *111*

They *112*

At All *113*

Goodbye *114*

Where I Want *115*

Poems of Love 116

A Peaceful Ending *118*

For Luke, To Remember You By *121*

Sonnet of Ocean's Mistress *123*

The god of the Night *124*

Only You *125*

Traffic *126*

The Beach *127*

Porch Swing *128*

The Portrait *129*

Tonight *130*

Endless Love *131*

Love Made *132*

Simple Love *133*

Just You *134*

Spell of Love *135*

Definition of Love *136*

Boardwalk *137*

Contents

The Hague 138

Distance Ballad 139

Winter 140

Promised Love 141

Dinner Date 143

Miracle of Love 144

Morning After 146

Unwed Promise 147

Fantasy 148

Passion 149

Late Night 150

Vulnerable 151

Dream 153

On my Mind 154

Question 155

Poems of Family

Beautiful
Understanding
Family
Nana's Song
The Attic
Remembrance
Our Road
Dad
Gramma
On Your Birthday
Childhood Ballad
Friend
Daddy
Not Forever
Concrete Poem for Mom
A Brother's Goldfish
The Fight
Support

Beautiful

The rolling red carpet of the Richmond hotel stretched from the sliding glass doors to the arched driveway several feet below, where my mom dropped me off valet-style. She insisted that I "arrive" in a chauffeured fashion in order to appear self-assured and important. Although I knew she wasn't being serious, my brother was less than thrilled at his role of opening my door. He smiled sarcastically, as he "accidentally" stepped on my foot and slammed the door on my skirt. My cover blown, I waited impatiently for my family to park the car and join me on the death row-like walk through the group of staring, gossiping and giggling girls flanking the registration area of the pageant.

Supportively nudged by an encouraging mother, I inched towards the check-in desk. Hormonal brothers scouted the excited contestants who dictated orders to bellhops, arranged their hair, adjusted their sashes and hugged each other in mock affection. I watched as several beauties bestowed the dramatic "air kiss" upon each other with as much warmth as a February snow. A few complete strangers squeezed my arm, exclaiming how lovely it was to see me again. I figured they must have been talking about a previous life, however, since I most certainly had never seen any of them before that day. Mock sincerity absolutely abounded, and it smelled like teen spirit. Actually, it smelled like Paul Mitchell hair spray, strawberry Lip Smacker and Obsession cologne. I felt faint.

Indeed, I had never been in a pageant in my life, and I couldn't believe I had decided to go through with this one. Although I was representing a small town, my sponsors were excitedly awaiting any news of success. In my case, representing a small place was worse than a large city, since the local newspapers, businesses and diner billboards made certain the entire population of my town knew I was off to capital to make a fool of myself. My sponsors said they were counting on my brains, talent and personality to bring home the coveted crown. On a limited wardrobe budget and minimal experience, however, I knew the crown was a long shot unless the majority of other contestants came down with a treacherously debilitating plague. In the absence of such a miracle, the best I could hope for was to finish the pageant without breaking my legs or busting open my head in a high-heeled fall.

The girls in this competitive lipstick circus were nearly professionals, many of them veterans of the circuit since they were babies. They were bold, brazen and beautiful with New Jersey hair, horse teeth and inflated breasts. It was Silicone Valley. I looked down at my own underdeveloped chest, noticing that some of the tissue I had stuffed inside my Maidenform Junior was sticking out of my collar. This, I thought, was only the beginning as I stuffed the sweaty paper back into my shirt, praying for humility.

My assigned hotel room was bright and spacious, and there were several vases of red roses waiting for me on the dresser from well-wishing relatives and friends. One of the two double beds already had Italian leather luggage perched upon it, so I heaved my plastic olive-green Samsonite on the opposite bed. My mom gingerly placed my hang-up bag in the closet and whistled at the sight of the expensive gowns hanging nearby. She looked at me apologetically and came to hold my hand. "You are going to look beautiful, honey," she said warmly. I smiled, rolling my eyes, and sat down at the oak desk to look at the weekend's itinerary. My brother pocketed the free hotel stationary and notepads, as I tried to figure out an excuse to go home.

Minutes later, as if my thoughts were being read, the best excuse for going home walked through the door. My roommate was six feet tall, blonde, and gorgeous, and her smile both lit up the room and dashed my hopes as she extended her hand to me. "Hi Roomie!," she said with Miss America poise and an adorable Southern accent. "I'm Beth, and I am so glad to meet you!!" Beth excitedly ran down a list of things she had already discovered about the hotel, girls she knew, what she found out about our pageant instructors, what was for dinner, as well as a dozen other newsbytes. I was surprised to find that she was honestly nice, and she seemed sincerely interested in me. Of course, I figured she was simply relieved that I was clearly not competition. Knowing that I was therefore not in direct danger of obtaining the rhinestone crown, I also relaxed, deciding that I would spend the weekend meeting new friends and just having fun.

Beth and my mom started to talk animatedly about hairstyles, as my brother fiddled with the radio. Suddenly, our chatter was interrupted, as Beth's mother burst into the room. I watched as her mother scanned my homemade dresses and well-traveled luggage. She scolded Beth for "chit-chatting" and told her that she had some mingling to do in the hospitality suite. Beth looked at me apologetically and nodded to her mom, who glared at my family, as they left the room. My mom, brother and I simultaneously looked at each other and burst into laughter. "Come on, darling," my mom said to me in a mock high-society accent, waving her arm in the air, "We have some mingling to do."

The hospitality suite was buzzing with activity. Manicured contestants, worried parents, frazzled reporters, and hurried hotel personnel were frenzied. I made my way through the crowd, occasionally stopping to say hello to anyone who looked inviting. I noticed that many of the girls looked worried or dazed, and I was suddenly more grateful than ever that my mom wasn't putting any pressure on me to win. Of course, considering the physical obstacles I had overcome in my life, I knew her only concern was that I simply not break an ankle. She just wanted me to have a good time. Furthermore, the months of practice prior to the pageant had been productive. I had worked on my posture, eaten healthy, and practiced my violin daily. It had been valuable discipline, and the resulting competition would be a learning experience in one way or another.

For the next two days, we were instructed by various pageant professionals on dance routines, songs, waving, walking, formation, the pageant process, how much time we had for changing clothes, what to eat, when to sleep and where to go. We learned the art of applying Vaseline to our gums to make lips slippery for constant smiling. We were given time to privately practice our talents and visit with family, before heading back to our rooms to reunite with our roommates.

At night, Beth and I were both relieved that our parents were not allowed to see us again until morning so that we could talk about the festivities and get to know each other. Beth told me that she had been competing in pageants since she was 4 years old and hated it. Her mom made her practice daily everything from walking to smiling and yelled at her for any imperfections or mistakes. Beth said she had already had her boobs "done" and had a couple of molars removed to achieve a more visible jawline. She said she envied my self-confidence and how easily I made friends. She said that most of the girls were talking about how sweet and fun I was and how they were going to vote for me for Miss Congeniality. Beth continued, saying that her mom would kill her if she received that award, because she was not here to be nice and that the only award worth acquiring was the crown.

We talked about the other girls she had been in pageants with for many years, the things they argued about, fights their moms had been in, and the amounts of money they have spent on dresses and lessons trying to "out-compete" one another. Beth looked weary and tired, but I thought she was an angel for bringing to my attention the beauty I had, the kind found on the inside.

After a half-hour evening beauty routine and several sleeping pills, Beth finally fell asleep. I hoped that she didn't spend the night dreaming of her place in society, superficial goals, an unending quest to be beautiful, and a mom who couldn't see that all she wanted was to be loved. I turned from watching this blonde beauty as she slumbered and stared out the foggy hotel window to the city lights beyond the grounds.

%   %   %

Days later, I lay sleepily in the back seat of our mini-van as my mom drove towards home. I held the trophy for Miss Congeniality in my hand, thinking that the greatest award was the acceptance of my family, the vote of my peers, and the comfort in knowing that I loved myself and was happy to be just me. So relieved to be going home, I kissed my brother on his cheek and smiled as he soured his face.

Understanding

Falling down

You try to make

The most of your goals

Running around

You still haven't found

What you want

But then

You call to say

Sorry for getting upset

Things aren't as

Planned—yet—

Don't worry about me

I understand

No need to apologize

Because I know

Family

As the fleeting glory of ones decisions
Mask generously the thought within
One ponders the reason for asking
Of that which hurts again and again
As the fiery heart in wickedness
Burns with passion and then with shame
The morning cinders at soul's hearth
Has only the tongue to blame
As the day of remorse gains to follow
The agony of pain melts away
Bringing a fountain of spirited understanding
And a beating promise of a new day

Nana's Song

Paper roses, faded valentines,
pinched cheeks, climbing vines,
statues of children, scented paper,
feathered pillows, feathered pens,
darkened wood, herbal tea,
flowered fabric, flowered dishes,
100 year-old china, polished Oneida,
wooden birdhouses, wooden floors,
musty lampshades, chipped rose bowls,
handspun cotton candy, braids with ribbons,
homemade ice cream, crocheted slippers, lace collars,
powdered skin, rose-scented lotion, straw hats,
tiny pleats, mirrored brushes, pressed flowers,
soft light, garden playhouse,
White Shoulders, white tablecloths, white aprons,
hand-dipped candles, tiny vinyl purses,
Sunday dresses, boys' grass stains,
towels for us, towels for guests,
cotton slips, pink bare feet,
jewelry boxes, hat boxes,
wicker sitting chairs, warm sugar cookies,
needlepoint pillows, latchhook rugs,
heart pendants, insignia rings,
drawers with beads, pockets with pennies,
pictures of memories,
countless patience, endless love,
what it must have been like,
Nana.

The Attic

Climbing
steps
to the attic
cobwebs
sticking
to my hair
searching
boxes
for old memories
photos
staring
at my tears
crying
silence
in sane agony
trunk
opening
through greedy dust
reaching
hands
explore
heirlooms
his calling
startles
my lonely travel
i keep only
a handful of dust

Remembrance

Like a leaf in a zephyr
I've been captured
If a breath I take
Could be sent to you
To prolong your life
And give us more years,
Papa, I could gaze into your eyes
Until the end of time
Never let me fall
Away from your legacy
Of Wisdom
And Power of your
Unconditional, Unfailing
Love.

Our Road

Our Road is at times shortened.
Our Path turns a different way.
We move our chosen direction,
Stepping further everyday.

Our Past may distress us and
We are reluctant to walk on.
We become weary from the pain
And stagger towards the sun.

Recollection can be impossible
Of what we've learned,
But we see friends have taught us,
And the joy and praise we've earned.

Diligence while we're walking
Becomes essential on our trek.
Our Road reserves many bridges
For times we must turn back.

Dad

Time swept through my life
Like a maddened breeze,
Blowing through childhood,
And stripping trees—
Looking back, I try to find
What it was I did wrong.
My heart only answers in
Hollow song—
Even in crises
When families find their worth
There are things we won't discover
On this earth—
Dad, I long to take your hand.
Say what I should've from the start—
Close your eyes
and try to hear
Words in my heart.
We'll fight the struggle,
Someday—
You know, I just want to say
I love you, Dad.

Gramma

All the memories that surround me
Tell me to recall
The good times and bad times.
The laughter or faults.
The times we were together,
The happiest known,
Mean even more to me
Now that I have grown.
The day we went our separate ways,
When I realized you had gone,
I prayed you would not forget,
I'll forever be holding on.
Sometimes I find it hard
Believing you're not here,
And I won't be seeing you
Year after year.
Every time I look up at the clouds
And see the rays shining through
It will always bring back memories of angels,
Memories of you.

On Your Birthday

October's leaves are changing
To November's reds and gold.
Timbers in the fireplace crackle
And woolen comforters unfold.
It's a special time of year
During the months of fall,
But today, Mother, the second,
Is the most momentous of all.
We celebrate your birthday,
A successful woman in time,
A mother, a teacher, a Christian,
And a loving friend of mine.
I want to express my feelings,
No clue where to start.
The words I write here
Hardly echo all in my heart.
You've shared much with me,
Your confidence upholding.
I still remember you holding me
When I was frail and unfolding.
The beauty of November
Doesn't hold a candle true
For a very special mother.
Happy Birthday to you.

Childhood Ballad

When all seems doubtful and faithless,
The end as imminent as e'er,
A woman, tearful, but hopeful,
Remained crying in her prayers.
Through days of unending struggle,
The child, vulnerable, but true,
From a woman's display of courage
Brought to life a breath so new.
The child, grown now,
From obstacles have been set free.
I love you and thank you, Mother,
For endless faith in me.

Friend

I look at you and see my strength.
I smile at you and sense your care.
I follow you and feel your pride.
I walk alone and know you're there.

I laugh with you and see your gifts.
I join you and hope for no end.
I pray for you and miss your laugh.
I look up to you
My brother, my friend.

Daddy

We lived under the same roof,
Yet we were thousands of miles away
And now that we really are
It seems like any other day
Have you really missed me
Now that we've gone our separate ways
Or has it been the usual
Work, more work daze
We both swore we were trying
Although it was hard to believe.
No matter how hard we tried
We never did succeed
Those years we hardly spoke
In the silence of the day
Before we reached each other
The hurt stepped in the way
Hey Dad, the past is behind us
If we let it be
I know remembering battles
Can injure you and me
I'm going to hold my chin up
Through whatever we may do
We need to start again.
I think you know that, too
Let's both try this time
When we've to Texas have flown
I have everything packed with me
But something is missing at home.

Not Forever

Sometimes we move so far away,
The miles seem so long;
It's hard to stay so very close,
It seems so very wrong.
Wrong we had to part and
Go our separate ways;
To write and think about
All our memorable days.
The days we spent that meant so much
To you and to me;
The days we would relive again,
Oh, all the fun we've seen.
It's our special friendship that keeps us close,
It didn't mean forever
Saying goodbye is always so hard
But a soul-sister's bond never parts, ever.

Concrete Poem for Mom

What are little girls made of? you asked.
Everybody knows
"sugar and spice and everything nice"
That is how the rhyme goes.
I got sugary on my first birthday, Papa said,
All spice first time I cooked.
I was quite nice in my Brownie troop, Mom said,
Gee, I remember how cute I looked!
I can remember the outfits you made for
Our cheerleader squad.
I remember our posing as sisters,
Oh! How everyone awed.
Camping, fishing, singing, crying,
Shopping, laughing, talking,
Times were never dull.
My years as that kid
Were the dearest of them all.

A Brother's Goldfish

Restless but quiet.
Same bright color as the sun.
Thinking not saying.
In a kingdom of his own.
Beautiful in his own way.

The Fight

Sometimes it's hard
To say what you feel
When a person won't listen
And you're both hurting still.
I wish we could
Be even just friends,
And keep everyone together
Before a relationship ends
Lost is a mere fragment
Of what we will be
If we don't sort problems,
And our feelings relieve
There are so many reasons
We may not ever know.
Why we can't just quit now
We've got too far to go

Support

Tears—

Cry away

Flood your heart

It wilts and

Snarls and frays

Cry away

I am here for you.

Poems of Fear

Winter Ghost
Dying
Nightmare
Attack
Abuse
Break Up
Crumbling Walls
Footprints
Tears
Long Distance
Ethiopia
Plea for Peace
Lonely House
Break in
War
Moon Shadows
FOG

Winter Ghost

All at once, the road looked familiar to me. Finally, I glimpsed into the past as I moved forward through the freckled snow. I remember these woods. I used to know them so well that I could find my way through them blindfolded as I played "Blind Man's Bluff" with my brothers. That was so many years ago but these woods evoked the memories. Oh, the hours we spent playing here. We made up games, played hide and seek, played Hansel and Gretel, and pretended we were in a fairy tale. Of course, having brothers also meant that I was occasionally a captive while playing war games, but mostly it was magical. As a teenager, my friends and I would walk down the paths sharing secrets and carving our names on the thicket. My sister and I would have tea parties between the thicket. As a young adult, I savored the tranquility of the paths to shed off the stress of the day or to cure the occasional migraine that now seem to come so frequently. I wondered if the paths still looked the same, and if I could find those carvings now.

My mind returned to the present as I turned into our two-mile drive-way, clearly marked by a brass sign on a gray brick pillar. The sign read "The Merewether Family," as the respective signs before the other drive-ways in the woods read with similar phrases. We were on the east end of the forest. There were four families, all owning adjoining parcels of the woods, in exact squares making up this block of the world. Our corner of the world, we used to call our area, was so close to the other families in the woods, the land seemed to belong to everyone. There were no fences, no borders, and no signs forbidding trespassing or bading to keep out. In the north, there were the Cambridge family, in the South were the Darling family, and in the west, the Talbot family.

Merely saying the name Talbot to myself made me remember what had happened so many years ago here. Mr. Ridgemore, a widower, whom we had all known for decades moved to Florida and sold his estate to a new family. I was already 18 and off to college. The new family, the Talbots, had five children, but I had never met any of them before I left for California. I had only that phone call from Daddy the year I graduated from UCLA telling me about the girl who had died in the woods. "One of the Talbots," he had said, "in a hunting accident, they think."

After UCLA, I had gone on to graduate school in Oregon and never did ask any more about what had happened, nor did my family offer any further news. I wondered if they still lived here. I wondered if they found out what happened and who did it.

My thoughts were interrupted by the sight of my mother heading back to the house with the mail in her hand. I couldn't believe I passed the mailbox without noticing it. I always notice mailboxes, it seems. The mailbox was a toy back then to us kids. We would leave notes for our parents in the box, and they to us. My father, on his way home from work, would slow down to a crawl and stop at the mailbox, languishing there so to give us enough time to become Robin Hood and the Merry Men and squander various change from his pockets under the threat of not his being able to pass.

My dad, ever patient and full of great stories, was our greatest playmate all of those years. My smile lingered at the thought, but then turned down a bit at the memory of his health and his age. He was older than most fathers when mom was pregnant with me. That didn't stop his enthusiasm or his energy, however, but I guessed that at 72 years of age, he would be a bit slowed down by now. Why did I take so long to visit, I thought. Before I could start feeling guilty, my mom turned around upon hearing my car down the drive. "She's here! She's here!," mom yelled to the house and turned to run towards me. Mom, wearing an apron, was rumpled and perspiring around her hairline. She looked like a frazzled cook who had been toiling in the kitchen for hours. I knew better, however, despite her efforts at being an effective housekeeper, that Cookie was behind the feast preparation underway inside. Cookie is the nickname I gave my housekeeper when I was two years old. A plump and boisterous woman from Jamaica, Tabita, came to us when I was born. Although she had been my nurse from birth, it was only when I was two did I ask her if she was my mom. I was not trying to upset or exclude my mom, of course, and at that age, I figured it was possible to have two moms. Both Mom and Cookie did equal parts in keeping the house under control, but when I asked Tabita, she said she was my nanny, housekeeper and cook. "Cook" was the only word familiar to me at the time, and I looked up to her proudly and said "you my cookie?" She smiled and nodded. So, from then on, she was Cookie.

I rolled down my window and yelled "Mom, get out of the road! You are nuts!" We were both smiling and she moved to the side of the road just enough so that I could pull into the drive. All of the sudden, from my back window, I saw the front door burst open and out flooded a dozen people. I smiled widely as I opened the door to the tender hug of my mom, and the various calls of "Sammy!," "You made it!," "Yippee!" and other greetings.

First to my side was my oldest brother, Brady, who was flanked by his two teenagers, Moira and Kyle. Brady smiled and said it was great to see me again. He seemed so grown up now, almost fatherly. How old did we all get so suddenly, I thought, as I smiled back to him. Next was my older sister Eleanor. She hugged me so tightly I felt my throat collapse for a moment. "Eleanor, Eleanor," I whispered. "It is good to see you too." I backed up briefly to use my fingers to say the words I had just spoken and Eleanor smiled. Precious Eleanor.

All at once Jack was behind me giving me a brotherly knock on the head and a bear hug. "Jack!" my mother yelled, "can you ever greet your sister without tackling her to the ground?"

Jack and I smiled at each other, as five Jack-lings came bounding to his side. I had been there for each of their christenings, which although did not seem that long ago, apparently were for the kids who stood around seemed huge. Katy, Zach, Mary, Kip and Zoe, all spitting images of their father and the wonderful brunette pixie he married named Dinah, who was waving from the porch with her hand resting on her round stomach. "My own football team," Jack joked, "Baby number six on the way, Sis!"

Brady punched Jack in the arm, Mom hugged Eleanor, and the kids linked arms with me. We all filed back into the house chattering and laughing, leaving the icy air foggy with our warm breath.

The house smelled like turkey, potatoes and apples, and Cookie bounded out of the kitchen wearing samples of each of these on her sooty apron! She took it off as she approached me, arms out and a tear in her eye. "My Samatty, my angel!," she cried. "Come over here and give me some love, child, 'bout time you get here." I hugged Cookie, wiping a tear from my own eyes. It was about time I got here. I was home.

I scanned the room as I broke from Cookie's embrace and she caught my eye. "He's upstairs resting, child." I looked at her in concern, and she squeezed my hand. "He'll be fine, Samatty, just resting old bones. Go and see him," she said, "He has been up all night anticipating you coming." I smiled and her and trotted up the stairs.

It was unlike Daddy to not be in the library if he wasn't on the porch or elsewhere in the house to greet me. I noticed upon entering the house that he wasn't in his easy chair, so I had a strange feeling that something was wrong. Cookie's comment made me feel slightly better, but I worried so much about Daddy. I worry so much about him not being here, I thought.

I paused in front of his door and knocked softly. There was no answer at my second knock, so I opened the door slightly and crossed the room. My father was resting quietly with a family quilt over him. He was so tall that his feet peeked out of the bottom of the blanket. I smiled at the sight, remembering all of the mornings I came into this room to crawl into bed with Mom and Dad and seeing his feet from under the covers. He was snoring lightly, and his hair was ruffled, and white, so white. Dad's hair was white, not gray, how did it get so white?

"Dad?," I whispered. "Dad? Dad?," I whispered again? I barely raised my voice, careful not to startle him. Daddy had always been such a deep sleeper, that the slightest loud noise would jolt him out of bed and start him out of the room. He was the consummate protector of his family, ready to bear arms and fight an intruder. We used to test him when we were little, making him jump out of bed, but as we aged, we realized that Dad was so tired because he worked so hard, and he needed his rest. "Daddy?," I said again and at no reply other than a slight pause in his snoring, I turned to go out of the room.

"Sammy?," Daddy whispered. "Button?" he said louder? "BUTTON!" he almost yelled, sitting straight up in bed and opening his arms. "When did you get here!!"

"Five minutes ago, Daddy." I replied. "I came straight up. How are you?"

"Well, I am old," Daddy replied, with a slight tinge of laugher in his voice, "but so glad to see you, Button. I want to hear all about how you are doing."

At the promise of catching up in the oversized library chairs after dinner, I got up to check into my room and Daddy went to the bathroom. I spied dozens of pill bottles beyond him but averted my eyes before he could catch the concern in them. I wandered down the hall until I found my old room at the end of the corridor. It was still as it always had been, filled with dolls and pictures, awards and memorabilia. Pink and lacy and smelling of lavender. Once I used to think this room was too young for me, but now I welcomed the teddy bears and pom poms. It was a nice change from the stark metallic walls of my apartment in New York, which had never seemed like home.

Over the din of dinner, the wind howled outside. It always amazed me that Mom and Cookie could manage to fit so many people in the house for a meal. The children sat in the kitchen around two tables, and the adults and teenagers were closely assembled around the dining room table. There was barely elbow room and the windows had to be slightly cracked as the temperature rose from so much body heat. Over the typical

Thanksgiving meal of roasted turkey, sweet corn, mashed potatoes, gravy, stuffing, yams and salad, we all caught up on our last few years.

The subject never came up, however, as to why I was coming home. As the youngest child, I was often the last to speak up, if I was not forgotten completely during lively dinner conversation, but I was surprised no one wanted to know. They were interested in Jack and Dinah's new pregnancy, Eleanor's new job, Brady's upcoming business trip, Mom's spa trip to Vegas, Dad's new chair, and the countless things to talk about and share with the children.

Eleanor signed from across the table that it was good to have me home. Those who knew sign language sang a chorus of agreement, particularly Dad who rose his glass and said "To Button."

The doorbell rang at precisely 9 a.m. the next morning. That could mean only one thing. It was Mrs. Darling. As if it were required to bear her name, she was indeed a petite, darling woman with a freckled face and a now gray bun atop her head. She wore bright colors and laughed with such spirit that it was nearly impossible to be in a bad mood in her presence. My mom was a firm believer that no suitable or properly-raised person would come calling, either by phone or in person, before 9 o'clock in the morning or after 9 p.m. She and Mrs. Darling went to the same grade school and finishing school as children and married best friends, so naturally, they shared many of the same ideas, a source of endless gossip between them.

Although I was struggling between sleep and awake, I knew my mother would be crashing into my room at any moment to throw back my curtains and sing an annoying good morning song. No one could argue that my mom was a morning person, but her songs and her antics put my siblings and I on the verge of throwing her out of the house many mornings in our past. Only Eleanor was also a morning person, but my brothers and I could sleep well past noon and think nothing of it. We liked to stay up past midnight reading books in the library with Dad, as he fell asleep doing the crossword in his chair. We played cards, chess, backgammon or just sat on the porch until we could force ourselves to turn in for the night.

I could hear Mrs. Darling's voice at the bottom of the stairs and knew at once that my mom would insist that I come and say hello. Before I was forced to be awake and "chipper," I stood beside my bed, stretched my arms, pinched my cheeks, swept my hair into a rubber band, and threw on my robe. I met my mom at my bedroom door and smiled, ever so slightly, plodding down the stairs saying hello to our over-enthusiastic neighbor.

"Oh Samantha," said Mrs. Darling. "We are so delighted that you might be here to stay a while. As you know Darcy will be home from Christmas, as will Paul and George. In fact, the boys are home now. I think your brothers went out for beer with them the other night." Mrs. Darling continued thoughtfully in the abstract, excited manner in which she always spoke. She would speak fast, then slow down, put her finger to her head a moment, pause, then continue. It was almost hard to pay attention to her words because her manner of speaking was so entertaining. "Anyhow, as you know George is *divorcing*," she whispered the word as if it were a secret or something terrible. Paul is still married with two kids. I believe they are the same ages as a couple of Jack's kids. Darcy, well, Darcy, you know. She is doing okay. She will be so glad to see you."

I smiled at Mrs. Darling as she ended and gave her a light hug. "I will be so glad to see all of them, Mrs. Darling. And, yes, I may be here a while." As I said that I looked over at my mom, who looked away slightly. I still had not figured out if she really wanted me to stay or if she was simply appeasing my father in doing so. They had always said that their home would always be open to any of us, no matter how old we were or under what circumstances, but something was different about her welcome now. I dismissed it for the moment and returned my attention to Mrs. Darling as she continued about the weather, a holiday concert in town, Mr. Cambridge's new dog, and if we had met the new hairdresser on Oak Street. As quickly as she had breezed into the house, she was back down the driveway, leaving behind a plate of cookies and fudge and a jar of homemade raspberry preserves.

I tightened my scarf around my neck and pulled a length of it over my lips. I scowled as I picked lint out of my Chapstick and replaced the scarf to keep the biting air from my lungs. The snow had slowed for now but it was to be heavier tomorrow. The ice would come tonight and by Monday when everyone hit the road, it would be a nice big mess.

I had left the din of conversation and chaos behind in the house for a short walk through the woods. I didn't expect to go far, but I had a searing headache and I needed some quiet. It was hard to find a quiet spot in the house with seven children milling around, and my father had been spending most of the day napping. He was thinner and paler than I remembered, but of course that was four years ago. I couldn't believe I had let so many years go by since my visit. I had seen them, of course, in Chicago at the baptisms of Jack's kids, but there had only been once since the last time I was here.

I must have turned while I was thinking to myself, as I ended up in a part of the woods, I didn't recognize. I wasn't lost, by any means, but curious as to where I was. As children, my brothers and the Darling children had been careful to mark many of the trees to guide us through the woods, but I didn't see any markings nearby. I walked several steps further and around a large tree. Suddenly, I was in a clearing. "I have never been here before," I muttered to myself. I caught a glimpse of something shiny in my peripheral vision. I turned and looked towards the ground where I saw a metallic post sticking out of the leaves. I bent to brush the leaves back and saw that it was a silver cross with a crucified Jesus on the front and a small medallion wrapped around it. I peered closer to read the medallion when I heard footsteps approaching. I turned to see sunlight around a tall dark shadow. I stood, quickly, sensing a danger I had never experienced in these woods. I turned, with the hair standing up on my neck, and ran towards home.

"What is wrong?" Eleanor signed in front of my nose, jolting me from my thoughts. I had not realized that even in the freezing weather, I had stopped on the porch and had been sitting in the swing contemplating what had just happened in the woods. "Why are you sitting out here?" Eleanor continued with her hands flying. She was concerned and shivering, and put her arm around me to guide me inside. She helped me with my coat and led me towards the fire in the library. I was immediately changed to see my father in his chair doing the crossword that I momentarily forgot about the figure in the woods, and the cross. The cross with the pendant. What was it doing there. My father looked up and signed to Eleanor that he was glad she found me and where was I and if she could perhaps get a pot of tea on for all of us. Eleanor left for the kitchen as I hugged Daddy, apologizing for being so cold.

"Where have you been, Button? We have looked for you everywhere." He said.

"Remember those headaches I get, Dad?" I said to him as he nodded. "Well, I had a bad one this afternoon, so I went to walk it off."

Dad sighed and nodded. "Walking gives me a headache now." He smirked. "And these holidays wipe me out." I smiled at him, the concern now starting to show at the edges of my mouth when I looked at him. He looked at me back, mimicking the concern. "I am glad you are staying, Button. It will make things easier for both of us."

I wondered what he meant, wondering if it were related to Mom or something else. I remembered the prescriptions on the counter in the bathroom and wanted to sneak upstairs to read some of the bottles. I didn't want to ask Dad about them because he would only tell me it was nothing. I didn't want him to gloss over an illness or a problem to protect me. He had always done that. I figured it was because I was the youngest. He would have serious conversations about various problems with my older siblings but as soon as I walked into the room, he was all smiles. "Buttons!" he would say, "Come sit by the fire with me and read." It was as if my entering made the problem remote and sitting by the fire more important, every time. We rarely missed a night in the library, even when I was a teenager. I would come in after a date or being out with my friends to my father pretending to be asleep under the newspaper or a book. After the first few times of attempting to sneak past him to the stairs to no avail, I would just enter the house and go right to him, and kiss him on the cheek.

Daddy and I had spoken on nearly every topic in that tiny room at the front of the house. There were also nights when we didn't speak at all. We simply stared into the fire to the privacy of our own thoughts, napped quietly in our respective chairs, or read books and magazines. When I was very young, I would get upset when my brothers teased me about being "a daddy's girl" or Eleanor called me "bookworm," but later I considered both a privilege. The reading had certainly lent to my success in school. I recalled now that Mom never seemed to happy about going up to bed without Dad. He would kiss her and say he would be up soon, but it would often be hours. I figured she really didn't mind, that she got used to it, but I wondered now if she figured he would stay up late with me again, like we did back then, and she would have to face sleep alone.

As my body thawed in front of the fire, I turned to Daddy. "I just had an unsettling experience in the woods." Daddy's eyebrow went up, beckoning me to continue. Eleanor came in with the tray of tea, making noises with her mouth, as she does from time to time when her hands are busy but she has something to say. She put the tray down and signed that I wasn't to begin without her. It was an enthusiastic sign language scold, and my father and I laughed at the sight of it. We all smiled.

Eleanor was a wonderful big sister to me. I had friends who literally hated their older sisters due to being victimized by sibling torture or other reasons, but Eleanor was always sweet and supportive to me all of my life. When I was born, Eleanor, who had been deaf since birth, asked if I could stay in her room in case I needed comfort. She said that she may not be able to hear me but if my crib was close to her bed, she could feel the vibrations when I cried, and she would go to me.

With Cookie, of course, I never really had time to fuss. I was always playing in the nursery, being fed in the kitchen, or on the floor of the library playing with toys. From an early age, I was at my father's feet, being read to, bounced on a knee, told I was special. I was actually the first of us to learn sign language, besides my parents. My older brothers didn't show much interest in Eleanor other than "base" in a game of tag or if they needed another player in a board game. I was fascinated with her from the beginning. She didn't talk, so she was never telling me what to do or scolding me, and I was fascinated by her hands as she signed to Dad or Mom. I don't remember how I learned to sign, but I learned and quickly. Eleanor and I would share countless secrets and advice atop her lavender canopy bed, or my pink four poster, and laugh and hug. We were soul sisters, literally, and I loved her.

Once Eleanor was seated, I began, speaking and signing that I had walked into the woods, seemingly turned in an unfamiliar directions, seen the cross in the ground, and ran back to the house upon seeing what I thought was a man in the woods.

Eleanor's eyes were wide and we both looked at my father for his insightful wisdom about the event.

Daddy didn't delay in responding, both speaking and signing. "You must have walked into the clearing where the Talbot girl died. I heard they have marked the area. That's their land over there, and you probably ran into one of the Talbots." Eleanor and I were both intent on Dad's explanation, and he continued. "It's my understanding that the Talbots aren't too fond of anyone out here. I guess you can't blame them since the case was never solved, but you would think after all of these years, we could all be a little more neighborly." Daddy stuck the pipe back in his mouth. The room filled with the scent of sweet tobacco.

Eleanor was full of questions. She frantically signed if I remembered what the stranger looked like, what did the cross look like, what else was in the clearing, did he say anything, did he follow me, what was he wearing, how far away was that area and was I scared. My dad watched as I signed the answers to Eleanor, and then moved his hands. "I think it's time that someone from our family go see the Talbots. I don't want to start feeling like we have to worry about boundaries on this land out here. Not after all of these years. I mean, it is terrible and all about what happened to that girl, and we are all sorry for it, but none of us did it, and we are being treated as if we should be guilty." Daddy continued. "Neither the Cambridges or the Darlings have ever had any pleasant exchanges with that family, and once Mr. Cambridge's old dog was shot at for wandering too far into the woods. I am not one to speculate or to accuse," said Daddy, "but the Talbots seem to be the only ones shooting guns around here."

Eleanor and I hung onto his every word and sat back in our chairs to let the meaning sink in. We quietly sipped our tea, enjoying the warmth of the fire, the aroma of tobacco and the tinge of mystery in the air of what was to come.

[Excerpt from "Ghost in the Pass," part of the short story collection in *Touches of Grace* by Shannyn Snyder]

Dying

A Mortal
you stand shaking before the Altar
of your bed,
Afraid
of climbing into Sleep.

Heavy
are your eyes which have not seen
Dark since last you fell.

The Lamp
now out of oil taunts Blackness
screaming, tormenting.

Wailing
you remain until a translucent hand
reaches out to lift you onto the
Mattress, cooling, calling,
soothing you to finally rest,
forever.

Rest in Peace.

Nightmare

the body float
in the river
we passed
i did not
want to look
twice,
Chicken,
they said
so I
checked out the
corpse
should we tell
the police or
pull it out
or let someone
else find it
later
figure it out
they called and
left me
with the bloody
rubber, gray man
eyes staring
at my horror
help me
he said
Crying.

I can't,
I whispered.
I can't even help
Myself.

Attack

Subconsciousness holds my hand as I run into the abyss again.
This is last night and the night before and a hundred nights.
I am running from him and that thunder drowning my ears.
Louder, I scream yet the thunder is louder.
Louder. Closer. Closer. Louder.
The brick wall.
Subconscious is gone…and my heart.
I am the abyss.
My arms rip behind me and there before me, Consciousness.

The mind is a riptide as I attempt to find the difference
between the two worlds I already know.
I struggle to find reality before it's too late
The forest spins around me as I fight this endless fate
Yelling, taunting and hissing, too damn many voices
My soul fades in and out, wincing in pain, mocking my choices
I reach out, nails like daggers, finding my sound
Sirens, whistles, blazing, redness all around.

Unconsciousness takes me again.
At least it's over now, and I'm alive.

Abuse

Terror roars within my heart,
Echoing through my soul
My mind stumbles with confusion
As the thoughts begin to roll
I watch his every movement
I catch his every breath
I look into cold, silver eyes
And feel the kiss of death
His words leave an impression
My mind replays it all
Still, I long to touch his body
Which made me feel so small
I could scream I hate him
He could beat me some more
Rather, I lay, my eyes shut tight
He stumbles out the door.
I am dead inside anyway.

Break Up

Do you see the hollow in my eyes

Gray like trembling skies

I hide the pain when I need to cry

Love dies

Crumbling Walls

The walls around me crumble,
And the Sea begins to rise.
Flashes of the darkened past
Spark briefly before my eyes.
I reach out for Comfort,
But find that no One's there.
A foggy Mist engulfs Me;
I retreat, running scared.
It seems too much to handle.
I don't know what to do.
I try to back Away and hide,
But then I run into You.
The Air then seems less ominous,
And the Darkness now seems to fade.
I can face my Weaknesses
Instead of Fading Away.
Don't change the Way You feel
If I express what is so True,
For a Wave of Emotion
Turns My teary Eyes to You.

Footprints

Footprints by the shoreline.
Teardrops from my eye.
A foggy December morning.
A light-gray colored sky.

A foghorn in the distance.
A gulls cry up above.
Mist hangs heavy on the boat docks.
No memories of love.

You left me standing all alone
I don't know where you are.
Where's the sunshine in this place?
How could you go so far?

So much of your life was left here.
I don't know what to do.
I cannot look at any thing
And help but think of you.

My life is not worth living
If you're not here with me.
I see our last footprints together,
Fading by the sea.

Tears

Rain drizzles down my window
Tears spill from my eyes.

Pictures of your gorgeous face
Glow against the skies.

Without you, it's not easy,
But living is not in vain.

I'll care for you forever,
And loving, I'll remain.

Then, memories seem to brighten
The ever-darkened skies,

And still your face is mirrored
In the teardrops from my eyes.

Long Distance

I am sitting all alone.
Silently. I watch my telephone.
The heavens scoff from up above,
Joking about our long-distance love.

There's a light by the setting sun.
Stars peek out one by one.
The moon awakes from his day-long sleep.
And mine begins to fall too deep.

My dream wanders to your face,
Looking down in warm embrace.
My hands feel a gentle caress
And all your loving eyes suggest.

Then, an open window fades in,
Reminding me of that day again.
The rays are shining faintly through.
You whisper you must leave me soon.

Tears fall to my pillow case.
Mirroring your fading face.
I waken to the traffic drone,
As the sun rises over my empty heart and
Home.

Ethiopia

Their land was as young as morning dew.

Now aged old as mountain crags.

There is pain, so much pain

That cannot be washed away—no rain.

They have bowls, but nothing to hold.

They must wait longer, they are always told.

How harder must they cry in the night

Before nightmare is overcome by healing light?

Plea for Peace

In the beginning,
There was Time…
From age to age,
It was wasted…
Now we're running out.
Soon, it will be gone.

Lonely House

Lightening flickers across the sky
the house shakes underneath
Thunder's loud command
Squirrels run to the woodpile
to find refuge as the rain
slowly steps onto the roof
The lamp beside me flickers
then blinks out as I watch
the Beauty of the Storm
I touch the telephone to dial
instinctively to reach you;
No matter how far away,
any moment is painful without you,
and I am scared now.

Break in

How do I know
whom i should trust
I'm hurting and
don't know what to do
what do i care
if they break down my home
they cannot vandalize
what is inside
of me
i need answers
no one will tell
i am confused at
what my friends say
smiles always covering
cynical grins
or kind words shading
betrayal within
what should i say
if they ask
to come in
turn away and shut
the door or...
i hope for the strength
to turn the other cheek
if they hit me once
they can do it again
i can keep my anger in
they fight my mind
yet i know their way

destroy everything
but I can pray
i won't change my mind
can't cheat my heart
stand by my beliefs
despite what they start
go mimic my name
rumor my needs
persecute my life
but I heed
they say they are friends
but i've plenty of them
i sort them out
i know where to begin
how do i trust
and whom do i see
is loving or caring
or is laughing at me
i'll follow my heart
then I'll be okay
i'll follow my soul
and stand in your way.

War

You know my name
whispered it before
if you knew my mind,
you would not whisper anymore.
the plan of our time
is the fault of their race.
I grin despite
anger on your face.
rain falls upon us,
sun dims in the sky.
our children will play
only by black light.
remember the swallow
or the white horse?
nothing we can do, brother,
please don't remorse,
should have discovered
long before now
there were no replacements
we don't know how.
if we don't believe
in hope for their world,
We'll only whisper the names
of our dying boys and girls.

Moon Shadows

In the darkness of the moon
I walked quickly in fear of night
Footsteps thudded behind me
And I jumped into the shadows to hide
Yes, I could see his form slowing
And studying the wind for me,
His prey.
He knew I was there, just not where.

I dared not let any warmth pass my lips,
Nor a blink or a shudder
He looked in the shadows
And then glanced away
There was someone coming
Causing him to leave
I muttered a prayer, but I knew
He would not stop.
He would come back.

FOG

Quietly creeps in.
Long tentacles strangling.

Gray evil smiling.

Air frightened quickly away,
Snuffing out traces of sun.

Poems of Faith

Why I Walk
Confusion
Calvary
Grace
Let Your Light Shine
We Will Stand
In Him
Symbol
Promised Land
Witness
Worthwhile

Mendez Middle School
English Department

Why I Walk

The air was misty and a little cool, and the courtyard at Hood College was a sea of excited people in white t-shirts, stretching and talking, introducing themselves and smiling. As I looked around at women with baseball caps and Nike tennis shoes doing jumping jacks and bending from side to side, I kept thinking that I shouldn't be there, that I was going to fail and disappoint my friends and family who were counting on me to complete this walk. What was a 30-year old who hadn't exercised in years doing attempting a 60-mile walk? The race was only for fit people, determined exercise gurus, people with more stamina who would complete each 20-mile leg over the next three days with ease and grace. There was no way I was going to finish this, no way to win.

The opening ceremonies of the Avon Breast Cancer 3-Day Walk were empowering, and the master of ceremonies said that there were people of all shapes and sizes joining forces to raise money through this event for a wonderful cause. He said that all of us were winners and that this was not a race, but a journey, one which we would each finish according to our abilities and that on this adventure we would learn something about someone else, and something about ourselves. He was right.

As the walk started, I kept in step with other walkers, smiling and greeting new faces, wiggling my toes in my slightly-broken-in tennis shoes that had seen me through six-months of training in preparation for these three days. As the afternoon wore on, the walkers (over 3,000 of us) started to scatter and pick one or two walking partners who were at their pace. By this point, I had seen numerous women who appeared to be in worse shape than me, who were older, or looked more tired, but as shooting pain seared my calves, I was reminded that I had another disadvantage that set me apart from this crowd. My legs were stiff and cramped, and this walk was a challenge for another important reason.

I took a seat under a large tree on the side of the path. Other walkers asked me if I was okay, and I nodded that I was "just resting a moment." Throughout the afternoon, I had become used to calls of "passing on the left, walker" and "are you okay walker" and "are you limping walker" or "why don't you ride up to camp, walker." Yes, I had been passed numerous times, but when I passed the last water stop, they called out "2,000" which meant I was not bringing up the rear, not just yet. I took off my shoes to inspect my new blister on my baby-toe and took at good look at my ankles. Each ankle has a scar that runs from my heel to mid-calf, one leg has a scar running up the side, with several more scars higher up my leg, and 2 more on my ankle. As I rubbed my calves, I silently cursed my ankles and asked God why he had to make it harder for me to walk than anyone else. I enjoyed the cool breeze for a few minutes, then realized that the walkers were thinning out again and decided to get back on the road. I finished that first leg around the 2/3 mark of walkers, and fell into my sleeping bag after a shower I don't remember and a meal I barely ate.

The morning of the second day made me sick to my stomach. I felt out of my league more than the day before and looked as if I had been hit by a truck. Other walkers were bouncing and stretching as if they had just come back from vacation, and more were excitedly talking about how fast the day before had been. I just glared and kept silent, trying to concoct a plan for dropping out with dignity, wanting to cry for my mom, and tell everyone who told me I could do it to stick it in their ear. I had raised over $4,000 for breast cancer, and perhaps that was enough and could be considered doing my part rather than completing the race. After all, didn't these people know what I had been through in my life? I had had more than 10 surgeries: operations that allowed me to walk, that made a crippled child finally skip and run and do all of those things that "normal" kids do, yes, I didn't need to be here, I had done enough. I was special enough as it was and had nothing to prove. I started towards the registration tables to ask if I could just volunteer in some other way for the weekend when I met "them."

Four women stood at the end of the mess tent, huddled in a circle rubbing their legs and chattering about tennis shoes and a sleepless night. As I walked by, they commented that I was limping. I muttered "I'm fine" and kept walking. One of them caught up with me and said "Hey, I'm Mary, are you sure you are ok?" I said, "yeah, just tired and I don't think I can do the rest of this walk." She said, "Neither did I, or did they, but I know we can." I sighed deeply, not ready for a dissertation about how they were all so out of shape when they clearly were more ready for the walk than I. Instead, Mary and her three friends shared with me, as we walked that morning, stories about their lives that brought me to tears and made me ashamed of the self-pity I attempted to mask as pride that morning when I had the urge to quit. One of them was a three-time breast cancer survivor, who had lost her breasts and most of her chest tissue. Another had prosthetic limbs, both legs, completely plastic. Another was a grandmother, who was raising her granddaughter because her own daughters, two of them, had died from breast cancer. The last one had no sweat glands was prone to overheating during exercise and had to be doused in water every five minutes. As I walked with these women, I thought about my own life, appreciating both the blessings and gifts I had been given, understanding that I was not weak or disabled, but able to be with these great women on this journey with each other and for ourselves.

For two more days, we walked together, sharing secrets and stories, laughter and tears. We clutched each other in pain throughout the final miles, and celebrated with each other at the end. At the 60th mile, at closing ceremonies, my family stood holding signs saying "We are proud of you" and "You Go Girl." My mom stood with her arms open, with tears in her eyes. We cried and held each other. This walk was not just for athletes. It was for me, and for others who did it simply because "we can." It was a walk for winners and a journey that turned pity into pride.

Confusion

Concentration is Impossible
Pray every Hour
Worried about School
Faith gone Sour.
Betrayed by a Friend.
Mocked by a Test.
Two weeks Remain.
God, I am a Mess.
Forgive my Wrongdoings.
Please help Now
I am starting to Fall—
Rescue me Somehow.

Calvary

I can't help but wonder
Why You died for me.
Whatever did I do
To receive the love I see?
Whenever I was weary,
You were always there.
You came and picked up pieces
Of a heart's despair.
Why did You take the cross,
And hang, for me, to die?
Should I feel Your Father's loss,
For in my soul, I cry.
I think about the thorns
They laid upon Your hair,
But even when they buried You,
I knew You were still here.
How could You die for me,
To hurt and suffer so,
To hang in pain for love,
And never let me go.

Grace

Silently you lay upon my lap,
Eyes closed in a dreamy nap,
I run my fingers through your hair,
Wondering not what thoughts lie there.
Tracing your lips which I may kiss,
Touching your skin my hands may miss,
I whisper softly a silent prayer
For the smile of God I've found here.

Let Your Light Shine

I have met many lonely people
Not long ago mirroring me
Before inviting Christ into my heart
Allowing me to see
Everyone here is changing
We're finding what truth can be
And the friend we find in Jesus Christ
Giving us reason to believe
I hope we will go and reach others,
And His love is seen in what we do
We we're placing our burdens
in His hands
So He can see our lives through
I am speaking through an open heart
I am praying through renewed soul
I gaze with a new smile.
Finally, in control.
Now I am certain
I'll be all God wants me to be
Standing up, to let my light shine
For the rest of the world to see.

We Will Stand

Satan wants us turn away.
Hammers us with temptations,
Nails us every day.
We tend to be caught at times.
Resistance begins to fall.
Forgetting God
Can uphold us all.
All efforts to destroy are in vain.
God's Holy World will always remain.
So hammer on,
Hostile hands;
Your hammers break,
but God's anvil stands.
Satan hammers such sorrow and woe.
Pain and toil can nail us on our path below.
Lord, grant that I'll never fail
Thy Hand to see
When the hammer falls towards me.

In Him

In His eyes, I find forgiveness.
In His eyes, I see compassion.
In His eyes, I see understanding.
In His eyes, I know love.

In His arms, I feel safety.
In His arms, I feel strength.
In His arms, I feel courage.
In his arms, I know love.

In His heart, I find bravery.
In His heart, I witness knowledge.
In His heart, I witness charity.
In His heart, I know love.

He, whose love is unconditional,
He, whose love cost His life,
He, who carries me when I am weak,
Has shown me the meaning of his love.

Symbol

I was walking on the shore
Of the Mediterranean sea.
I was thinking of a place
Where more might be done for me.

I saw a lonely man
Sitting upon a rock.
I was glad I wasn't him.
I wondered if he'd talk.

I really wanted to keep going.
I had "important" things to do.
I stopped-guess I was curious.
He did look blue.

I smiled and said, "Good Morning."
He looked up in surprise,
Smiling as if I were the greatest thing,
A sudden brightness in his eyes.

He reached out a wrinkled hand,
And gave me a small clear box,
Containing a grain of sand.
He got up from the rocks.

I watched him as he walked away.
I held the box in my hand.
I was thinking of my selfishness,
And my fantastic plans.

I guessed the gift was a symbol
Of the love that I can share
With those who need just a little.
All it took for his smile was care.

The box is on my dresser,
And when I begin to demand,
I forget myself and remember
He who gave me the sand.

Promised Land

I wanted to go somewhere
  I'd never been.
I wanted someplace
  New to stand.
I closed my eyes and
  Wished upon a star
To go to the promised land.
I opened my ears to
  A doubtful chorus.
There was no land
  Of promise.
I had tied my heart
  To a star,
But it didn't go
  Very far.

I felt my heart
  Sink very low.
I was letting all
  My dreams go.
I needed someone
  To go with me.
But, I couldn't
  Really see, ~

That all I needed
  Is my sweet Jesus
To love, and guide,
  Help, and need us.

I'm going to look
    Up to the Father.
And my dreams
    Will go much farther.

So, if you're looking
    For the promised land,
Allow the Father to
    Grasp your hand.
He wants to reach out
    To each of us,
Have faith in his
    Son, Christ Jesus.

Witness

I have this aching in my heart.
The hunger is why it could have start.
Did I have all that life could give
Getting so much harder to live.

But, I get up and fight,
As something inside was holding tight.
I was scared, I could not see—
Someone special was calling me.

I took a chance and heard His plea.
He opened His arms and hugged me.
I rose and smiled, let go the fight
Became a soldier in His light.

Worthwhile

I want to express my feelings,
But I wouldn't know where to start.
The overwhelming emotion of love
Seems to overflow my heart.

You have shared so much with me
Your confidence has held mine.
I thank you for all you've taught me,
Now all I need is time.

I'm going to give my all to Him.
I'm going to try my best,
I'll tell Him I love Him and mean it,
And all that you suggest.

My ride here may get lonesome,
Or full of err and trial,
And though love doesn't make "the world go round"
It makes the ride worthwhile.

The way to love anything
Is to realize it could be lost—
But I'm willing to fight until the end
No matter what the cost.

Thanks, again, for bringing me closer
To the One I most love.
You will be greatly rewarded.
I'll see you up above.

Poems of Hope

WWII's Aging Heroes
Eden
Stained Glass
Trusting You
My Future
Overseas Flight
Lighthouse
See This in Me
Heaven
The Unicorn
Ready
Together
One Day
Destroyed Love
Save the Children
Coming Home
From a Soldier
Tortured Heart
A Prayer
Safe
Granted Taken
Dedication Enclosed
Tell Me
Forget It
DIVERSION

Metamorphosis
It's Late
Sunrise
Wonderful
Race
Waves
Poverty
They
At All
Goodbye
Where I Want

WWII's Aging Heroes

Lawrence Raymond Davidson, born in Plymouth, Kansas in 1919, was the eldest son of a crop farmer who dreamed of one day becoming a commercial pilot in California. That day would never come, however, since in 1940 he elected to take the place of his drafted but disabled brother, Cliff. Lawrence spent the next five years with the 17th Wing as a bombardier on a B-29 in the Army Air Corps in the Pacific campaign of WWII. He was young. He was brave. He is my grandfather.

Papa recounts for me the years in WWII, from close quarters on the bomber to friends who died from enemy fire merely feet from where he stood. He remembers the time he spent defending our country vividly, despite the time that has passed. Papa keeps letters and souvenirs from WWII in a box on the china cabinet. He keeps the memories of fear and confusion locked in his mind, and is forever grateful that his plane was never hit despite the dangerous missions they pursued. Papa adds that he is grateful that he was never captured and able to go home and that there were so many soldiers who did not or could not return.

Over the past few months, I have spent some time talking with Papa, asking him questions about the war, reading letters he kept from relatives and those returned to him after the war had ended. He remembers happy reunions with friends and celebrations at the USO, but his letters also describe the pain he went through as a young soldier, not quite sure what he was doing so far from home, armed with weapons and courage.

I have always been patriotic and proud of those who served and continue to defend the United States. As a former military dependent and close grandchild of my Papa, I adopted a conservative view of defense and honor those who have the courage to fight for the freedom of others. Last year, I arranged for a White House flag to be flown in Papa's honor, for the years he spent defending our country. I remember the tears of appreciation and joy as he sat in his San Diego home and opened that box I brought from Washington, D.C.. He read the letter from President Clinton, thanking him for his courage and dedication. I am so proud of him.

Further, as I read the hundreds of pages I have collected on this war, I am captivated by other stories of hope and pride. It is my absolute hope that the soldiers of WWII are never forgotten, that their memory will always live in our history, that we will memorialize their strength, and that they will forever be regarded as heroes.

Eden

Never had I realized, the garden where I
played as a child was so indicative of emotions
I entombed within my heart. Let me retreat so that
I may imagine your smile again. Through the winding
fern my wheelchair became entangled. I slipped
down and began to crawl as the branches and stems
whipped my face, until I reached my place between
the roses. The flower as a whole was magnificent
to behold, you, I guess I could say with your
consuming eyes and elegant poise; I have now
found a rose to look at and become fond of as time
elapses. In the anguish of the week, the vines
grew quickly while I found intrigue and invited
fantasy into my thought. The plant reached out
to the soil. The beauty built. With every
moment I welcomed another treasure, another gift,
in your uplifting smile. However, the vines increased,
and they wrapped my arms and legs and waist. I felt
the soft petals of the rose as they brushed lightly
against my cheeks. Every stem danced towards me
to introduce the sacrifice, encouraging me to you.
I met you and saw your redeeming eyes up close.
I plucked a few scarlet shells and noticed the beauty
was also contained within.
With each impulse, I am bewildered at my thoughts of
you. Now, as I place a fragile velvet lip into my
pocket, my own whisper that I shall return to this
Eden to adjoin our dreams once again.

Stained Glass

Only a simple painted window
Filled with pieces of glass, colors,
Changing.
    And then

Through the glass, peering, I
Stand bewildered at images unseen,
Hidden.
    Yet then

Poetry is as Endless as lectures
On the Epistles when written
Uninspired.
    For when

Embodied upon my mind are
Shades of color painted by
Sleeplessness.
    And when

Beyond deep swollen eyes
Lie affection for the dust of stars
Enveloped.
    For you

Like a leaf in a zephyr I am
Captured by your breath in a
Repetition,
    Only you

And your eyes flash as colorful,
Warm, as a child's innocent laugh,
Unexpected.
    To Me.

Trusting You

Only a whisper of love's countless efforts
Ventures forth from my lips
In a gesture once true
Of all the meaningless uttered solicitudes
Thrust from elsewhere the heart
In a manner overdue.
It can be only the power of wanting or
Mere dreaming of passions
Which bring me to you;
And I dare not mutter in earnest confusion
Of the deepest center of heart
Lest my weakness show through.

My Future

When I look at you, I see sincerity
and honesty unabashed.
As I look at you, I see the future
designed for our dreams.
When I think of you, I feel my desire
fill me with wonder.
As I think of you, I am full and
blessed beyond belief.
To have you is to have the world
finally at my fingertips.

Overseas Flight

Sometimes we try too hard
To break away
And spread our wings.
When it comes time
To return,
Things have changed.
I hung my head
And cried.
When I returned,
You had gone.
You left something
On the ground
Below me.
I picked it up
And held it
To my heart,
A piece of you,
A small token of
Your love.
A fragment from your heart—
You were asking
Me
To wait for
You.

Lighthouse

When clouds begin to gather
Over distant lonely skies,
I grow weary of the battle
And the storm I walk towards.
When all around is madness,
There is no safe point in view
I long to turn my path homeward
And spend some time with you.
When life becomes a battle
Or as barren as Winter's skies,
There's a beacon in the darkness
In a distant pair of eyes.
In vain I search for honor
And in vain I search for truth,
But these things can still be given
Your love has shown me proof.

See This in Me

Full moon
Over the water
Waves glisten
In your eyes—
Look at me.

Gulls above
Glide to nests
Songs ring
In your ears—
Listen to me.

Strong will
Falling down
Towards the clouds
Covering you—
Reach to me.

Fire in your eyes.
Pain in your ears.
Terror in your mind.
Fault in your heart—
Call to me.

Countless tears
On my pillow
Prove to you
All that matters
Is you and me.
Do you understand now?

Heaven

Is there another moon?
Is there another sun?
Have I another heart?
Own I only one?

How could one only be
If you've stolen mine from me?
Am I holding yours?
What do your eyes see?

I see clouds of heaven.
I see rainbows before rain.
I see foams from every ocean.
I see fields from every plain.

The stars are glowing brightly,
Never to be dimmed.
The breeze is blowing lightly.
I'm thinking about him.

My candle has burned to nothing.
Soft wax has overflown,
Like the love that fills my heart,
Never broken, never sewn.

Was that a drop of rain?
Or a teardrop from my eye?
Was it a falling star?
Or a comet across the sky?

Absence makes a heart grow fonder.
I'm with you in my dreamland.
The golden sand glistens beneath us
As we walk, hand in hand.

The Unicorn

Clear fragile statue
Cradled in your hands,
Symbolizes the peace and
Hope
You bring to
My life.

Small innocent animal
Brings magic to your touch,
I held him in
My arms;
I miss you
So much.

Tiny lifeless legend
Cries out to your heart,
As I did when
I kissed
The horn
Of the tiny
Unicorn.

Ready

It takes just a little while
To find your way.
It takes just a little more
Than one night and day.
Past memories will not go away.
It becomes harder to strongly say
I'm ready to go on again,
Ready to be more than friends,
Ready to live,
Ready to love,
Ready to belong to someone again.
I can heal.

Together

I stare at the sky and think of

How far away you are.

Yet you seem so close and maybe

We stare at the same star.

The aster shoots like a rainbow

Across the summer sky.

Maybe the moment was shared

Across the miles,

Together, you and I.

One Day

The rolling of the foamy waves,
Powerful and arrogant blue.
The song it whispers reminds me
Of a dream that must come true.

Being here without you
Is not pain, but
Being here with you in my heart
Really is not the same.

One day we can be together
For as long as we may.
One day I'll be with you forever.
I look forward to that day.

Destroyed Love

Yesterday, two lives

Overflowing with despair as

Waves destroy weakened shores.

Remember, it takes faith in

Love to repair what

Love destroyed before.

Save the Children

Bullets fly; white flags rise
Inside our hearts—
Another war.
Hands shake; blood flows;
Our salty tears
Now pour.

A crippled man, blinded child,
Both in the likeness
Of me
With staggered words,
Blinded heart; a victim
In an innocent sea.

Nodded head, outreached hand,
Each battle will be
Fought and won.
Time turns old signed
Pages of trial.
Our chapter has only begun.

Coming Home

Everywhere is silence.
A dark shadow swallows air.
I crawl into my deepest thought,
Wishing you were here.

I do not know where you are,
Have you lost your way?
I drift, I float, dreaming,
As night draws into day.

Though I try, my heart grows dimmer
For those who weakly roam.
I hope they see the distant light,
So they may finally come back home.

From a Soldier

I sit by my barrack window and try
To peer as far as my eyes can see,
But the gloomy shadows of city streets
Allow only the reflection of me.

I see myself, a young and lonely soldier
Who dares to call himself a man,
Though he clenches his teeth from crying
As he holds pictures in his hand.

I glance at the portrait of my family,
Smiling proudly at their son,
Who pledged his life to patriotism
And battles to be fought and won.

When my ambitions gained me no honor,
My family still supported me,
Although the years are lengthy,
I know they're waiting patiently.

As I reach to place them on the sill,
One behind it slips and falls.
Bending down to gently rescue it,
I find it hard to stand so tall.

I see others outside walking
Alone under the starry blue night.
I realize if I were with her,
Everything would be alright.

Can't she see why I feel defeated,
As I vision her white wedding gown?
When I finally am able to claim her,
She may no longer be waiting around.

If only she knew how much I love her
And how I long to touch her hand.
Oh, the heart holds so many torments
Which even torment cannot understand.

I try to hold my composure,
But the tears only wildly fall.
I hold her portrait against my heart
And try to resolve it all.

I lay in my bunk and dream of
How badly I need to win, and
How I pray she'll still be waiting
When I face the day again.

Tortured Heart

It must seem very frustrating
To understand my many thoughts
As evening shadows courageously dance
Through ivory curtains to play;
Your softened, handsome features glow
Magnificently in the brilliant blue light;
Peace overcomes the warming house
Where so beautiful over love endures,
Remaining as you leave for the day,
And I anxiously await your return,
Each moment builds us, near or far,
Your spirit within me although you're gone;
I recall every word and action
And every gesture of strength towards our dream;
I offer countless nightly prayers
For your goals, happiness and pride,
Longing for the day you come home to me,
I must not leave your side;
Every moment of my life is for you.

A Prayer

Tall
you stand
even though
you sit and
I see
strength
in words
not said
nor heard.
Power
I sense
within our
friendship and
Trust
I know
finally, yet
without test.
A blessing unto
my hardly—
deserving soul.
You,
a friend
only moments
ago a dream.
Tightly
I hold
onto hope—
Aspirations
you desire

shall unfold.
You
Will never fall.
know that I
Will
Always
Be
There
As
You
Are
For
Me.
Thank God for you.

Safe

Quickly

I fall

into a

shadowed

abyss

Screaming

I echo

your

name

Smiling

I enter

your arms

Sheltered

I am

safe

again.

Granted Taken

Time

is important
to hold onto
when you're
uncertain

how long
fortunes will

remain in
your
hands or
treasures

in your midst.

Follow your
dreams as
they

appear and
never let

go of
your
blessings.

Dedication Enclosed

If I could paint a portrait
Of the way you make me feel,
The painting would be cast in motion,
Yet portray all time stand still.
If I were an artist, polished;
I could blend and shade and mount.
I could color each inch of canvas
For the meaning you are about.
If I could paint a symbol of you,
I would need those for love and trust and grace.
I would want an honest, open reaction,
Perhaps a trace of tear upon your face.
If the portrait turned out even close
To the image I had planned and dreamed,
I know I would sense your pride,
And a little hope would be redeemed.
As of late I feel the need
For quiet symbols to be portrayed.
Indeed in each distant moment,
There is only warmth sadly masked and delayed.
As a tall ship fighting the often warring sea,
I know there will be testy waters for you and me;
But all barriers can be overcome, rewards received,
If you love in symbols and actions and always,
always believe.

Tell Me

If you smile at the thought of touching my hair
If you shake at the thought of touching my hand
If you tear at the thought of losing my trust
If you dismiss the thoughts because you love me too much
If there will never be more than a casual call
If there will never be help whenever we fall
If you cannot live without having me near
If you need to find that your feelings are true
I'll tell you my secret if you tell me yours too.

Forget It

does not matter
if you do not
understand me
I'll never ask for anything
never will I
expect you to give
I know you are
afraid
if you feel you
do not deserve this
never mind
if I could only
hear you say
you love me
I would break down
and cry
you feel it, I know
you are so scared
to let it free
I will never let
you go
if it were
tomorrow
that we had to
say goodbye
I know I could see
love in your eyes
my hand would be beside you
my heart would

touch yours to
guide you
no matter how
you fight to
avoid giving into
your pride
I see through
your bitterness
I see love
and I return
always
to
you.

DIVERSION

Dancer
Graceful   Fragile
Gliding Striding Whisking
Leaping Turning Spinning
Awkward Clumsy
Athlete

Metamorphosis

Day
Sunny, warm, lively
Smiling, dancing, singing, delighting
Melancholy, waiting, moaning, frightening
Dark, cold, quiet
Night

It's Late

It's late and I can't sleep.
There's a thunderstorm outside
I'm all alone and frightened,
And there is no where to hide.

Everywhere I see shadows,
Noises taunt my mind.
Lightning casts an eerie glow,
Not one comfort here to find.

Somewhere a voice is calling,
"Do not be afraid"
and "If you look you will find comfort,
from a far away charade."

Suddenly I see a brightness.
The worst of the storm is through.
The comfort I found in darkness,
Was the memory of you.

Sunrise

Glowing claws outreach.
Grasps dark shadows in her hand.
Rules in shared domain.

Wonderful

The sky is becoming dark now,
But I don't see the gray.
The air is becoming colder,
But I whisk my coat away.

It may be thund'ring and lightning,
But with…you there's no storm.
It may be freezing and tempestuous,
But with you, I am warm.

The days are getting shorter,
But I've all the time I need.
Everyone's locked in themselves,
But, I can be me.

They'll be running out of time,
With you, I've got forever.
They all may be stuck and trapped.
With you, I'm free as ever.

Ever since I've met you,
The world's more beautiful ev'ryday.
I notice things I haven't before
Have they always been this way?

Life is just so wonderful,
Grass evergreen and sky everblue.
The world is ever at its peace.
And so am I with you.

Race

Life is a great race,
You and I are the runners;

The race must begin, and
Somewhere it must end;

To all who are fair,
There's a prize at the end;

Life is a great race,
You and I are the runners.

Waves

Perpetual strength.
They roll into the incessantly waiting shore,
And then back to the mystic sea endlessly.
I want to remain here forever.
All around me is unruffled and tranquil.
There is no disturbing noise or distracting movements.
It's just me, the immortal ocean,
And the everlasting sound of the rolling surges
Of tremendous strength and power.
I want to remain here forever.
I am thinking.
I see a valiant gull courageously skim the violent waters,
My troubles and fears wash away with every wave,
Mended with love and serenity.
I am myself here.
I want to remain here forever.
Independent, serene, full of perpetual mystery and wonder.
I am not merely just a child here.
I am unique.
I want to remain here forever.
Close your eyes and join me here.
It's one more thing to share.
You won't ever be lonely,
And you'll want to stay forever.

Poverty

We can't go on so ignorant
Thinking their hunger's a bluff
They can't go on long alone
And tears are not enough
Feed the people
Cure their pain
They're our family
Treat them the same.

They

They know not why there is none;
They know not why it is all gone;

They know not if their children will live;
They know not if the world will give;

They know not how to live their days;
They know not how to find more ways;

They know we can calm their fears;
They know we can share more than tears;

Why don't we soothe the pain they feel;
Why don't we try suffering for a meal.

They've done it for years.

At All

My cheeks are stained deeply
From flowing tears
Which yet have not ceased
These lonely years.
Sorrow fills my weakened heart,
Stressing the piercing, biting pain.
I know you may be out here,
But it isn't really the same.
I won't forget all those memories
We made in Oregon.

Goodbye

I wish I did not
    have to go today.
"Good-bye" is such
    a sad thing to say.
I didn't want to
    break down and cry,
But its hard when
    it's time,
For saying "Good-bye."

        The seagulls are crying,
            with their heads hanging low.
        They know it's time for
            someone to go.
        It won't hurt as bad
            if we find a way
        To meet again one day.

Hold your chin up
    through whatever you do.
You're going to go far
    because I believe in you.
Yes, "Good-bye" is such
    a sad thing to say,
But, we'll meet again—
    yes, again, soon, someday.

Where I Want

I'm where I said I wanted to go.
I'm where I wanted to be.
I'm discovering things I never knew,
And seeing everyone I wished to see.

I never thought I'd make it here.
This place seemed so far away.
I'm here now,
But I do miss you
More with each passing day.

When you are ready, though,
Come join me here—
I will wait for you.

Poems of Love

A Peaceful Ending
For Luke, To Remember You By
Sonnet of Ocean's Mistress
The god of the Night
Only You
Traffic
The Beach
Porch Swing
The Portrait
Tonight
Endless Love
Love Made
Simple Love
Just You
Spell of Love
Definition of Love
Boardwalk
The Hague
Distance Ballad
Winter
Promised Love
Dinner Date
Miracle of Love
Morning After
Unwed Promise

Fantasy
Passion
Late Night
Vulnerable
Dream
On my Mind
Question

A Peaceful Ending

Frantically, I ran to catch the ringing phone, bashing my left hip against the sharp edge of the kitchen counter. Wincing, I struggled to catch the answering machine, but it had already finished recording. Pressing the lit "play" button, I heard a soft deep female voice quietly say, "I didn't want to leave a message, but I thought you should know that Luke passed away yesterday. We are having a quiet family ceremony. It's what he wanted. Call us next week if you want to talk. Bye."

The plastic receiver dropped from my palm and crashed against the paper-strewn desk in the chaotic study. My gaping mouth hung, dry and immobile, suppressing the ache in my throat to wail. My stiffened body swayed in shock as powerful memories flooded my mind, passing through like a speeding train. Oh Luke.

In front of my eyes flashed every moment with him, and there had been so many. Luke and I met at the end of my freshman year at the University. I had just landed a position as an advisor for the following year, and Luke was assigned as my mentor. He was Italian, tall and lanky, yet slightly muscular from squash. His toothy smile could charm a snake, and he was brilliant. We would stay up late in Acacia Dorm's study lounge, talking about politics and current events, sharing poetry, discussing mythology and occasionally stealing a timid kiss.

Like many college-born relationships, neither of us took our feelings towards each other too seriously. I, especially, guarded myself from being heart-broken by men, and Luke was a dramatic flirt. He was known to be "experienced" with women, and our two Taurean personalities often caused lightning to flash during a disagreement. Luke and I did, however, share a special bond that he did not find in his empty relationships, and between "optional dating," we would often return to the beacon of comfort we found in each other's understanding.

Luke, like me, began his fragile life in a neonatal care unit, artificially pampered by tubes and wires. We remembered names of kind nurses and medical procedures and agreed that our strength and energy came from the miraculous gift of life we cherished. We wisely concluded that asking for immortality would be punishably selfish. We accepted endings.

Dating Luke was an unusual experience for me, and I knew that he allowed me to see a part of him that no other woman ever did. It was the part of his life that included life support systems, complicated medication and his struggle to live with advanced cancer. The Florence Nightingale part of me was happy to be a nursemaid when he wasn't feeling well enough to shuffle around his dorm or go to Chow Hall for a meal. The other part of me, the little girl who had grown up in countless hospitals, losing friends to terminal illness, would often find myself wanting to never again be near anyone ill. My desire for Luke and the challenge of being his "constant" relationship, however, gave me the staying-power to love him, through his tantrums and treatments.

Sleeping beside him, I was always conscious of his breathing. I would often stay up until morning watching his stomach rise and fall, pressing my ear lightly against his chest to see if the gurgling of liquid in his lungs was worsening. Chemotherapy was the ghost I would fight when he relented. I would check his forehead every few hours to make sure he wasn't burning up, and I would quickly cover his frail body with blankets if there were a hint of a shiver. For a year, I was his everything, and he was my validation that someone needed me.

I remember on one cold December night, Luke slowly turned to me and said, "I love you, but I have nothing to offer you. You know I'm sterile. You know I'm on fifteen types of medication. My life expectancy was up long ago. I think we should end this thing between us before it gets too hard to handle." He shuddered and looked at me, with tears in his eyes and whispered, "I am finally dying."

What happened after that soliloquy fogged my mind. I remember him dressing in a cloud of silence, despite my vigorous protest. I think I insisted that I wanted to be there for him, with him until the end, whenever that would be. He simply said no and left, forever this time. I tried to call him a few times after our parting, but eventually gave up. It was what he wanted, and I moved on with my life.

Startling myself out of my catatonic state, I stiffly sat down in my desk chair, reaching to hang up the fallen phone. In slow motion, I buried my head in my hands and loudly sobbed for Luke. The tears enveloped the pity I carried for our failed love and the relief that his struggle with life was finally over. The painful coughing, gasping for breath, and fight for one more day was finally rewarded with the gift of eternal life. It was a granted prayer for an end to pain and a promise of a new peaceful beginning.

*Names and situations have been changed to protect privacy.

For Luke, To Remember You By

Soft evenings of Sanborn, of Berlioz, of Lanz, and of Luther,
of dancing candlelight, of white wines and sautéed mushrooms
of philosophy books, of thesis papers and poetry manuscripts, of
    countless colleges,
of rackets and meditation, of slippers and robes, of incident
    reports and in-services,
I have all of these memories, but nothing of yours to remember
    you by.

Endless days of wistful calling, of speaking to machines,
of old and new numbers and new names, of old debts and old
    debtors,
of old ghosts and of new ones to come, of doctors who are
    friends, of mothers who are scared,
of shared graces and grace, of gray walls and given gifts
I have all of these memories, but nothing of yours to remember
    you by.

Dark nights of your coughing, of my fear of your sleep, of
    hours of straining to hear,
of your breathing, of truest love and purest passion, of kisses and
    knees weakened,
of old medicines and new therapies,
I have all of these memories, but nothing of yours to remember
    you by.

Misty mornings of my walking, of my praying and my
 hoping,
of a great hero and a greater man, of life that is longer before it is
 longest,
of paring goals and careful promises,
of the wholeness in your eyes which were windows to your heart,

I have all of these memories, and
It is I who has everything of yours to remember you by.

Sonnet of Ocean's Mistress

The ocean's sun wakes from its sleep,
Dark mists of night drift away,
The creatures sleep still, while they may,
The tide at its ebb, may it keep;
The sea's spell of sleep is so deep,
As though it might drift away,
Sweet singing is heard from the bay,
Our parents wake from the deep,
The gulls glide low to hear,
Soft ringing embodies morning in awe,
The mistress of Poseidon's ocean
Protects small creatures from fear.
She watches closely each tiny creature
Who roams the glory of her bedroom.

The god of the Night

The scarlet of your tender lips
Brush softly o'er my breasts and hips
Your Body warmly shadows mine
As Night draws till the end of Time
Cupid's arrows pierce my heart,
Where esoteric passions will to start
With deep of kiss consumes my skin
And your Breath erases all fear within
Through toil and fear, fire and rain
The Beauty of Our Love remains
And as each Chapter begins to fill
I pray the armored Sands of Time lie still

Only You

Your deep kiss warms my lips
Your warm touch thrills my skin
My body is eager to wrap you
In the love I hold within

Each day my passion builds
And I wait in earnest hope for you
My heart fills with cautious strength
As I count down, another day through

Never have I honestly needed
Or wanted so much so true
To give everything
To any man, only you

Traffic

Too many faces
To many expressionless faces
To name any passions
To name fateless passions
Too many promises
To break yet another promise
To hear one answer
To hear one honest answer
From your lips
From your precious warming lips
That's all I need in this Hell.

The Beach

Mighty
trembling of the
misty waves
casts a phantom
into the black
light of the heavens
songs of passion
breathe closely
on my aching skin
and powerfully kiss
my thankful hands
and Time
echoes its rhyme
over the youthful
spray as his
body falls gently
upon mine
casting a blanket
of white foam
on our drumming
embrace while my
fingers drop from
his beating ivory flesh
and slip into
the cold lips
of the crystal sand

Porch Swing

When I lay in your arms last night,
My body float in peaceful flight.
The moonlight cast a shadowed beam
While kisses flowed in gentle stream.

Complacently, I wonder what to do
As my body fills with the warmth of you.
Each touch lingers past the next;
At your side I lay, transfixed.

Each second counts, but comes too soon.
My heart sinks as you leave the room.
In tranquility I speak my love for you
As you walk away in the morning dew.

The Portrait

I sit apprehensively,
Awaiting the finished
Piece
The curiosity of
Wondering what lies
On the canvas
Overwhelms me.
I wring my hands.
The alacrity of
The artist's wrist
Carefully streaks
Washes of color
Across the
Paper.
I think of you
And smile,
Hoping the portrait
Mirrors the peace
You give me.
I miss you.
The painter retraces
His work;
He forgot the simple
Tear in my eye
From dreaming of
You
While I am here
Waiting.

Tonight

Carry me away
To the cradle of your arms.
Take me away
To the secrets of your heart.
Find a way
To free me from this pain
Of wondering when
I'll see you again.

The day gets longer
But I hold on.
The day gets longer
But I am strong.
The day gets longer,
But it's nearly night.
When the day is over
I'll hold you tight.

Hold me close
It seems so long.
Hold me close.
I'm holding on.
Hold me close
So I can savor your touch.
Don't let go
I need you too much.

Endless Love

Poetry becomes Endless
In Epistles of Love
I've carefully Written
For you.

I attempt to Write
Different Verses
For Songs We've both
Sung true.

Embodied upon my
Mind are Shades
Of Color painted
By Love.

Beyond deep Eyes
Lie Affection for
Millions of Stars
Enveloped.

Stroll into My Poem
My heart welcomes
Your Presence forever
Unlimited.

Love Made

Introspective,

I wonder

How you

Are able

To Move

Me

Like the Wind

Moves the Tide

Under the Surface

Of Poseidon's Sea.

In your Hand,

I'll abide.

Touch my

Palm

To feel

Magic through

Your unclothed

Body.

Simple Love

All I want to say
Is I'll think of you today.
I'll kiss you
And hug you
And whisk you away.
I'll feel you
And hold you,
Touch you,
Behold you—
Never, ever,
Want to you stray.
I'll breath you
And think of you
All day,
For I love you
And need you.

Just You

Beyond a whisper,
Beyond a doubt,
Beyond your touch,
I live without.

Beside your body,
Beside your skin,
Besides your soul,
I live within.

Beneath your breath,
Beneath your eyes,
Beneath the clouds,
You warm the skies.

Spell of Love

Every time I look at you,
My heart spins around.
I reach out to touch you
Yet, I utter not a sound.

Everyday I spend with you,
I realize I am blessed.
I wish you could see inside
At all my heart suggests.

Every moment I think of you,
I grow a little stronger,
Knowing if I pray faithfully
I can hold out a little longer.

Every kiss I send to you,
And words of love I whisper
Only cite a fragment
Of love I yearn to vesper.

Definition of Love

I drown in your shadow.
I wander in your light.
I wait patiently by day
To lay beside you at night.
You tug at my mind.
I melt at your touch.
I'm under a spell;
I need you so much.
I'm hypnotized in your eyes
And I'm falling apart.
I'm mesmerized in the skies
Of your heart.
Alone in your strong arms,
I'll never be the same.
I've memorized all of you.
How am I to blame
Feelings between us sent
From heaven above
In an insane emotion
Dreamily defined as love.

Boardwalk

Here we sit on the docks alone,

Hand in hand.

We need no words.

Evening breezes whisper by,

We hear the coo of seaward birds.

Gazing into your loving eyes,

I'm at peace.

I need just you.

An endless night

In your arms;

These feelings true.

Waves calmly wrinkle by

Under our stars.

I'll love you

Forever….

The Hague

Peering out my dorm window,
I anxiously await your return.
Mixed feelings of impatience and pleasure
Seem to zealously spark and burn.
Fastidiously, I recheck my hair
And merely spray perfume.
Before I stand sentinel again,
You quietly entered the room.
Throwing wanting arms about you,
I eagerly kiss your lips.
I yearn to hear your soothing voice
As my adoring heart lay fixed.
In your eyes I become distracted
From elements of a troubled world.
Soft touches impulsively excite me
As I lasciviously unfurl.
Your fervent skin pressed upon mine
Calms much deeper than the soul.
Your sensual contact lingers, but sigh;
I realize you really need to go.
Across the brief miles I focus
While loneliness and sadness deprive,
For I understand how blessed am I
To care for you. I love you.

Distance Ballad

Sensations I hold within me
Torture my fragile heart.
I long for you to hold me
And touch lips I softly part.
As I wistfully dream of touching you,
I stare into engulfing eyes.
My body freely melts away,
Wishing you lay by my side.

Hold me now in your own dreams.
Hold me inside your vivid mind.
Take me now into your gentle arms,
Hold me, until the end of time.

Gazing beyond my lofted window,
I see you walk below.
My body becomes impatient
While my aching skin glows
I attempt to calm and compose,
Yet, this never seems to do;
The moment you take me into your arms,
I realize how much I missed you.

Winter

Shadows hide in cold winter
Nights.
Autumn's slow leaves hesitate in
Flight.
Worn graying stars smile, but in
Tire.
We settle comfortably before a cedar
Fire.
Thanksgiving is past, Christmas
Awaits.
Wonder engulfs me as I arrive
Late.
Carolers melodious drift joyfully
By.
Rooftops awaken to snow laden
Skies.
To you I offer a year of
Grace,
To delight my eyes on your loving
Face.
I ask only that your faith remain nothing but
True
And to forever remember I love only
You.

Promised Love

Again today, my mornings are yours,
And the hopes and dreams that dawn in their light.
Again today, my dreams and gratitude are offered,
For my gift to you is my life.
I will always remember when you first called me
Out of my empty sleep
To awaken in me the essence of faith
And love I needed to find.
A treasure like you is so rare,
Like a solemnly granted prayer.
You gave me your life as a sign of trust.
Strengthening with the smile of every day.
You believed in this ambitious woman
Whose eyes overflow with praise.
You overlooked and forgave my failings,
Only asking of me to try.
Albeit you are miles away,
I can feel you nearby,
And I enter the glowing pride of day
With burning embers delighting in my soul.
You are the fresh rainfall whom offers this seedling
The chance to tower beneath the sky.
Weightlessness enters my body
Requiring only a single casual glance.
Riches are insignificant armor.
I promise today to sing for the world
A song of praise for you.
The ides of tomorrow will swell with sounds
Of the love within my spirit.

You are beauty undisguised
    And unlimited in your giving.
Again today, my mornings are yours.
    My dreams have blossomed in your light.
Especially now, I thank you
    For being the greatest gift to my life.

Dinner Date

your eyes sparkle in the dim
of the restaurant
the waiter smiles at us
while we search the menu
i reach across the table
to take your hands
somehow I am no longer hungry
i only long for the courage
to kiss you now.

Miracle of Love

How do you
make light
in the darkest
of night
or the brightest
glow
in bitter cold
snow?
How do your
eyes sing
in the harsh
ringing of rain
or your spirits
raise in the
most tormenting
of days?
How did I
receive such
a blessing
as thee or earn a
miracle
so personal
to me?
How do you
feel as you're
holding me
still or
kissing my lips
until our

hearts both
refill?
How do I
love thee—
it's been written
before,
but I love you
forever,
and even more.

Morning After

Mist
sneaks into my room
silently
kisses my sleepy eyes
open
to see only darkness
wishing
you slept here tonight
spirit
uplifted to the moon
prayer
answered each moment
blessed
by your love and
touched
in your heart now
fog
retrieves the dampness
replaced
by your breath
warming
Me.

Unwed Promise

No need for
a ring on my finger
to be sure
I alone belong to you
No need for
a ritual favor
to believe we understand
unity as one
after all these years
No need for
permission
to hold you and love
you the rest of my life
you know I need you
don't forget this
I live for the doors
To your precious heart.
No need to
mention every minute
that I promise to be
forever loving and loyal
As I believe
you'll feel it
from me, Always.

Fantasy

Night—

Every color of the spectrum

Combined—

Making love to you

Paradise—

Our bodies intertwined

Fantasy—

Crowds of stars still shine

Morning—

We still have time.

Passion

I lie here watching
you undress before my

aching skin. A cold
room once, now steam.

Moonlight teases my
eyes and runs across

your chest and hips.
I reach to take your

hands into mine. The
room becomes scarlet,

then violet, passion has
color. Inside, I scream

in silence, intimacy has
language. I float, I swim,

I weave, I scratch, I yell,
Quietly. The midnight air

explodes. Love has scent.
Your arms are hot on my

body, always replaying the
warmth you fill me with tonight.

Late Night

As my eyes burn

From tears of tire

I wonder how long

Dreams shall aspire

Doubt comes in

Yet walks back out

Nerves jump inside

My mind will shout

I hear your voice

On the telephone

My spirits climb

I long for home

Soon I'll be

Near you everyday

As your love washes

Every tear away.

Vulnerable

Forgive me for feeling weak
Forgive me for climbing steep
Forgive me for diving deep
I cannot resist
Forgive me for wanting you
It isn't what I meant to do
But every time I look at you
I cannot resist.
It's the power of love
You have over me
It is the warmth I feel
When you touch me
I melt away
It's the fire in your eyes,
Makes me hold on tight
When your skin delights on mine
I float away.
Forgive me for watching close
Forgive me when I boast
Forgive me when I dote
I cannot resist
Forgive me for following you
It's not what I'll always do
But when you whisper I love you
I cannot resist
To see a thousand stars
Resting under us
A bridge over passion
We always seem to cross

And I know that you're aware
When you rest your gentle head
That I eagerly await
To satisfy your demands
The moment you hold me
To send a fragile kiss
I rise and fall like heaven's clouds,
I cannot resist.

Dream

No one try to wake me
From this dream of mine,
I never want to leave your arms,

Until the end of time.
How come I remember

The color of your eyes
I never dream in color,
But mainly grays and whites.

Is this a reality
I think it's too good to be true.

Only in a fairy tale
Could I fall in love with you.
I thought I was dreaming

And it stood against the skies
I looked at you and saw

Those destined soulful eyes.

On my Mind

Every song on the radio
Says something about you.
Always reminding me
Joyous and blue.

I seem always to be dreaming,
My attention turned to you.
You may be hundreds of miles away,
To me, you're within my view.

I can't remember when I was happier,
Or a time that I could find,
When I went through an hour
Without you on my mind.

Question

Too many troubles and woes.
For all I've asked and suggested
Nobody ever does as
Anyone's requested.

But, let me get an ear in here,
Let me make a suggestion…
If love is the answer
Could we ask a different question?

0-595-27187-1

Printed in the United States
142403LV00004B/2/A